copy & cut

Animals

Paul Johnson

A & C Black · London

First published 2002 by A & C Black Publishers Ltd
37 Soho Square, London W1D 3QZ

www.acblack.com

ISBN 0-7136-6235-2

Copyright project ideas © Paul Johnson, 2002
Copyright illustrations © Kirsty Wilson, 2002
Copyright cover illustration © Alex Ayliffe, 2002
Editor: Lucy Poddington
Designer: Kim Sillitoe

A CIP catalogue record for this book is available from the
British Library.

A & C Black uses paper produced with elemental chlorine-free
pulp, harvested from managed, sustainable forests.
Printed in Great Britain by Caligraving Ltd, Thetford, Norfolk.

Contents

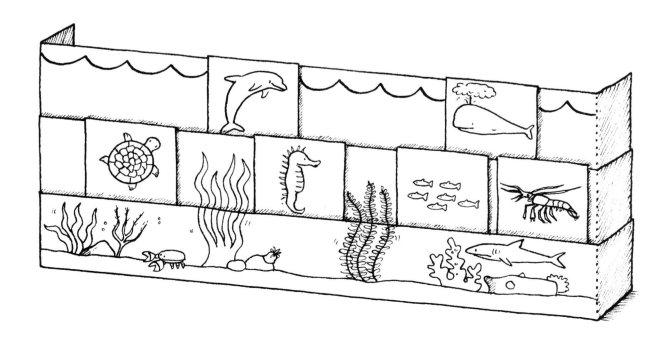

Introduction

How to use this book

Copy and Cut: Animals provides a wide variety of photocopiable craft templates, each with simple instructions for children to follow. The templates enable children to make books and models which link to the science curriculum objectives for learning about animals. The projects also provide innovative contexts for practising writing and literacy skills. There are opportunities for the children to read instructions and write text for a purpose, including non-fiction texts such as reports and descriptions.

The projects are designed for six to eight year-olds, but many are also suitable for younger children. Any project can be easily adapted to your needs by masking and/or substituting text. Favourite templates can be removed from the book and filed with other relevant resources. At the back of the book, you will find notes for teachers which include practical suggestions and additional information on the project themes.

Preparation

First pull out the template page and cut around the border. Use this master page for all future photocopying. (For a more exact copy, lay the page on the photocopier plate rather than feeding it in.) To begin a project, photocopy both sides of the template for each child and check that the necessary resources are available (see 'You will need' for individual projects). Introduce the theme and discuss ideas for the project with the whole class. If necessary, read the instructions with the children and demonstrate what they mean. It is particularly useful to show the children how to hold the page to start with. A photocopiable page of helpful hints is provided on page 60.

Decorating the projects

The templates can be reproduced on white or coloured paper or card, either as A4 or enlarged to A3. The latter is a particularly useful size for demonstration purposes and projects which involve substantial amounts of writing. The instructions suggest only basic decorating materials, such as coloured pencils, to avoid requests for materials that may not be available. However, it would be useful to start a collection of extra resources, so that children can be more adventurous with their decorations. Suitable materials include glitter glue, pearlised paints, metallic pens and paper, coloured foil paper, sequin mesh, tinsel, holographic paper, art straws, sweet papers, wrapping paper, magazines, fabric and wool.

Tips for good results

Encourage the children to try out decoration ideas on a piece of scrap paper first, and to plan in pencil. It's a good idea to avoid the use of fibre-tipped pens, as colours may run through the paper. If you copy the template onto card, show the children how to score along the dots with a pencil and ruler before folding.

You could consider making two copies of the template for each pupil. One can be used for the rough draft and the other for the finished piece. Children could word-process texts and stick them on to their finished model or book.

Ideas for display

These projects are perfect for school displays. Why not mount projects together on a classroom wall or in the school hall? Take the class on a nature walk and display projects about animal habitats alongside the children's drawings and recounts of the walk.

Mammal misfits

A mammal has a warm body and a backbone. Mammals can be furry, hairy or wrinkly. They might have sharp horns, big flapping ears or a long wiggly tail. There are two mammals already drawn in this flap book. Draw some more, then mix them up to make crazy mammals!

You will need: the Mammal misfits template • scissors • pencil • pencil crayons for decorating

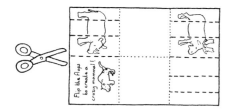

1. Cut along all the dashes.

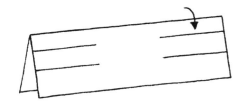

2. Fold the paper in half lengthways, with the pictures on the inside.

3. Fold the flaps with the moose picture to the middle.

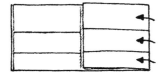

4. Fold the blank flaps on top.

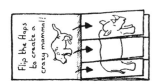

5. Fold the flaps with the rhino picture to the middle.

6. Fold the cover on top of the rhino picture.

Open the cover of your book. Then lift the rhino flaps one by one. Mark on the flaps underneath where the rhino's body joins up. Draw a mammal on these flaps, one part at a time — head and front legs first, then body, then hind legs and tail. Check that your picture lines up with the rhino picture.

Draw another mammal underneath the moose picture. Colour in all the pictures.

Write a title on the cover of your book. Now mix and match your mammals!

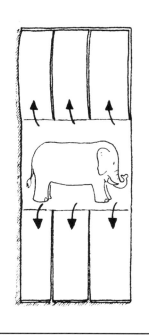

Flip the flaps to create a crazy mammal!

True or false?

This will help you to find out more about animals. Discuss with a friend what you know about different types of animals. Write a question which begins 'Is it true that...?' Use books and CD-ROMs to help you find out the answer. Does your friend agree?

You will need: the True or false? template • scissors • pencil • pencil crayons for decorating

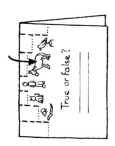

1. Fold the paper in half widthways, like this.

2. Cut along all the dashes.

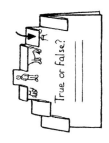

3. Fold forwards along all the dots. Then fold backwards. Unfold.

4. Tuck all the flaps inside, like this.

Write your question on the front of your card. Try to find out the answer. First think of animals which seem to show that it is true. Then see if you can find any which prove it false. Write the answer on the back of the card. Decorate your card by drawing some of the animals.

True or false?

Riddle book

You are going to make a book and then write animal riddles inside. Choose an animal. What is special about it? It might have horns or antlers. It might have a long beak or fierce teeth. Use your ideas to write a riddle about it. Can your friends solve the riddle?

You will need: the Riddle book template • scissors • pencil • pencil crayons for decorating

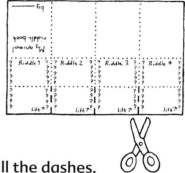

1. Cut along all the dashes.

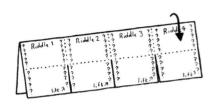

2. Fold the paper in half lengthways, like this.

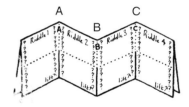

3. Fold the paper in a zig-zag along the dots (A, B, C). Start by folding forwards along the A dots.

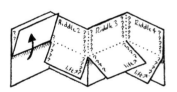

4. Lift the flaps and fold them along the dots.

Write your first riddle in the book. Give clues about what the animal looks like and what it does. Then lift the flap and write the name of the animal. Draw a picture.

Choose three more animals. Write riddles about them on the other pages. Don't forget to decorate the cover of your book!

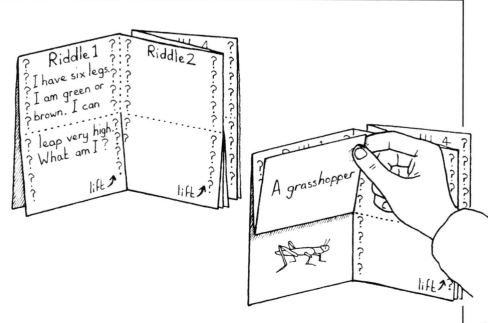

Ocean creatures

What animals live in the ocean? Think of animals you might see near the surface. Then think about what might live further down. Can you think of any creatures that live on the sandy bottom? Use this scene to show where different animals live.

You will need: the Ocean creatures template • scissors • pencil • pencil crayons for decorating

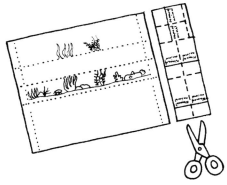

1. Cut along all the dashes. Put the strips to one side.

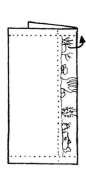

2. Fold the paper backwards along the A dots.

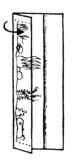

3. Fold the paper forwards along the B dots.

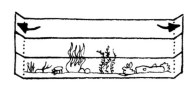

4. Fold the paper backwards along the C dots.

5. Draw ocean creatures on the strips. Use the longer strips for the creatures near the surface. Use the shorter ones for creatures further down. Write their names below the pictures.

Colour and decorate your ocean scene. Draw the waves at the top. You could draw more animals, such as sharks, seahorses, crabs or jellyfish. Slot the strips into your scene where they belong. Move them around to bring your scene to life.

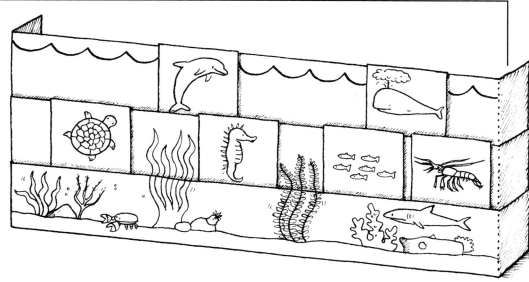

13

A   B

C

A

B   A

C

Name of
animal:

Name of
animal:

Name of
animal:

Name of
animal:

Name of
animal:

Name of
animal:

Growing up

Many animals change a lot as they grow up. A frog starts life as a tiny egg.
Then it becomes a wriggling tadpole. The tadpole slowly grows
legs and becomes an adult frog. Show the stages
of a frog's life on this model.

You will need: the Growing up template • scissors • glue • sticky tape • pencil •
pencil crayons for decorating

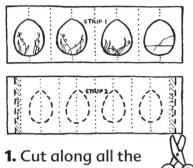

1. Cut along all the A dashes.

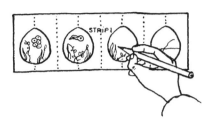

2. On Strip 1, draw a different stage of a frog's life in each window. Draw them in the correct order.

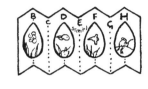

3. Fold Strip 1 in a zig-zag along the dots (B, C, D, E, F, G, H). Start by folding forwards along the B dots.

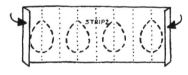

4. On Strip 2, fold the 'glue here' tabs forwards. Unfold.

5. Fold Strip 2 in a zig-zag along the dots (B, C, D, E, F, G, H). Start by folding <u>backwards</u> along the B dots.

6. With the paper folded, cut along the dashes. Open out the strip.

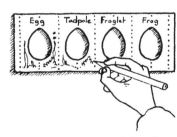

7. Decorate the <u>blank</u> side of Strip 2. Write labels above the windows to match the pictures on Strip 1.

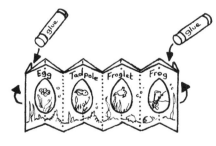

8. Spread glue on the tabs and fit the two strips together, like this. Press the glued parts together.

Tape the glued ends together to finish your model.
Tape a piece of thread to the top and hang it up.

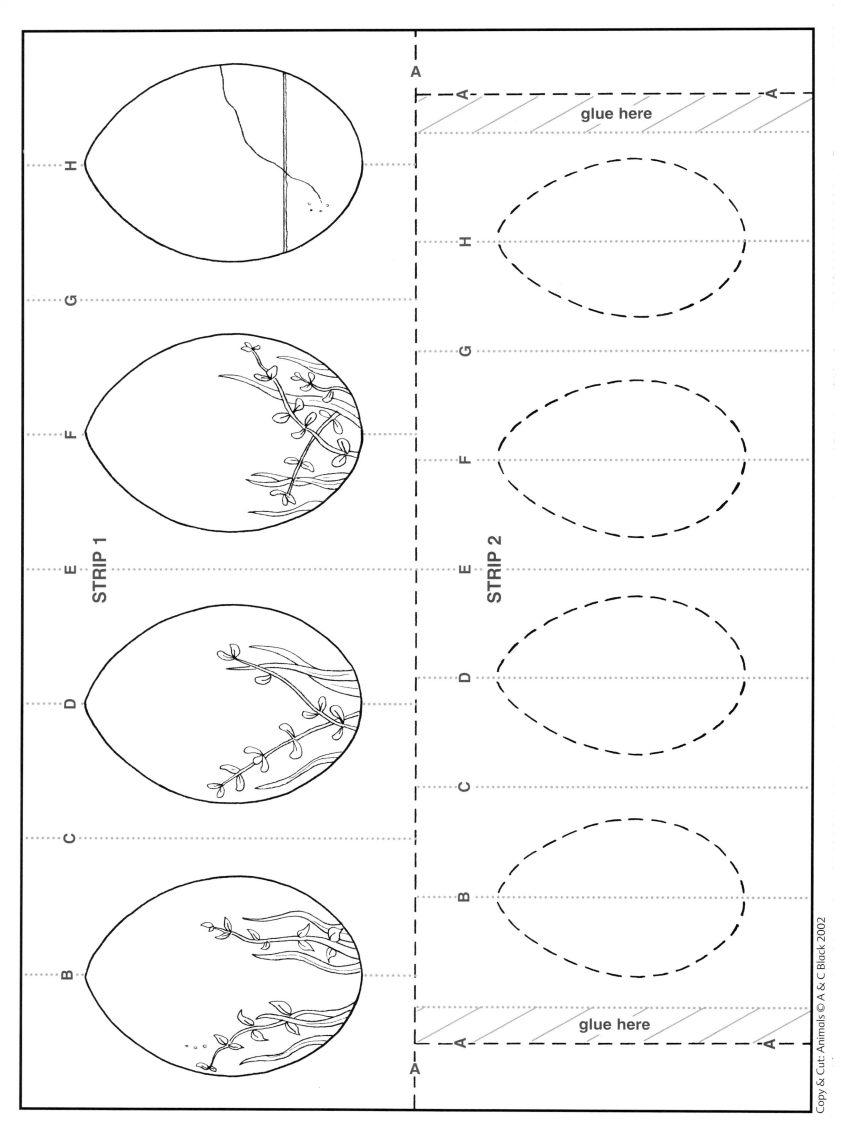

STRIP 1

H

G

F

E

D

C

B

STRIP 2

A

A glue here A

H

G

F

E

D

C

B

A glue here A

A

Snake mobile

Snakes belong to a group of animals called reptiles. A snake has rough, dry scaly skin and no legs! It moves by curling and wriggling its long, wiggly body. You are going to make a snake mobile. Look at pictures of snakes and decide how you will decorate your mobile.

You will need: the Snake mobile template • scissors • hole puncher • a length of string • pencil • pencil crayons, coloured paper, fabric and glue for decorating

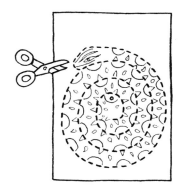

1. Cut along all the dashes.

2. Use a hole puncher to make a hole in the circle.

3. Loop a length of string through the circle. Tie it in a knot.

Write a poem on the blank side of your snake. It could be about snakes. Think about the way they move, the sound they make and what their skin might feel like. Or you could write a poem about the way different animals move.

Decorate the other side of your snake with coloured pencils. You could cut shapes from coloured paper or fabric and glue them on.

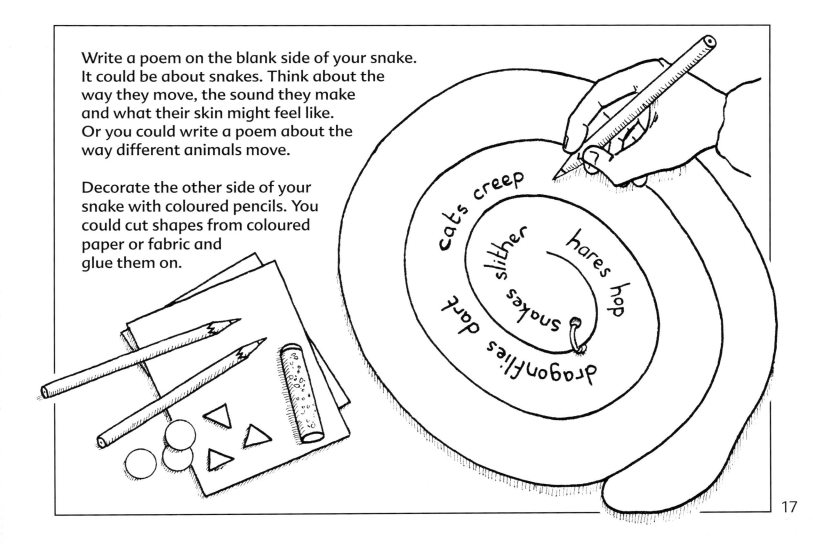

cats creep
hares hop
snakes slither
dragonflies dart

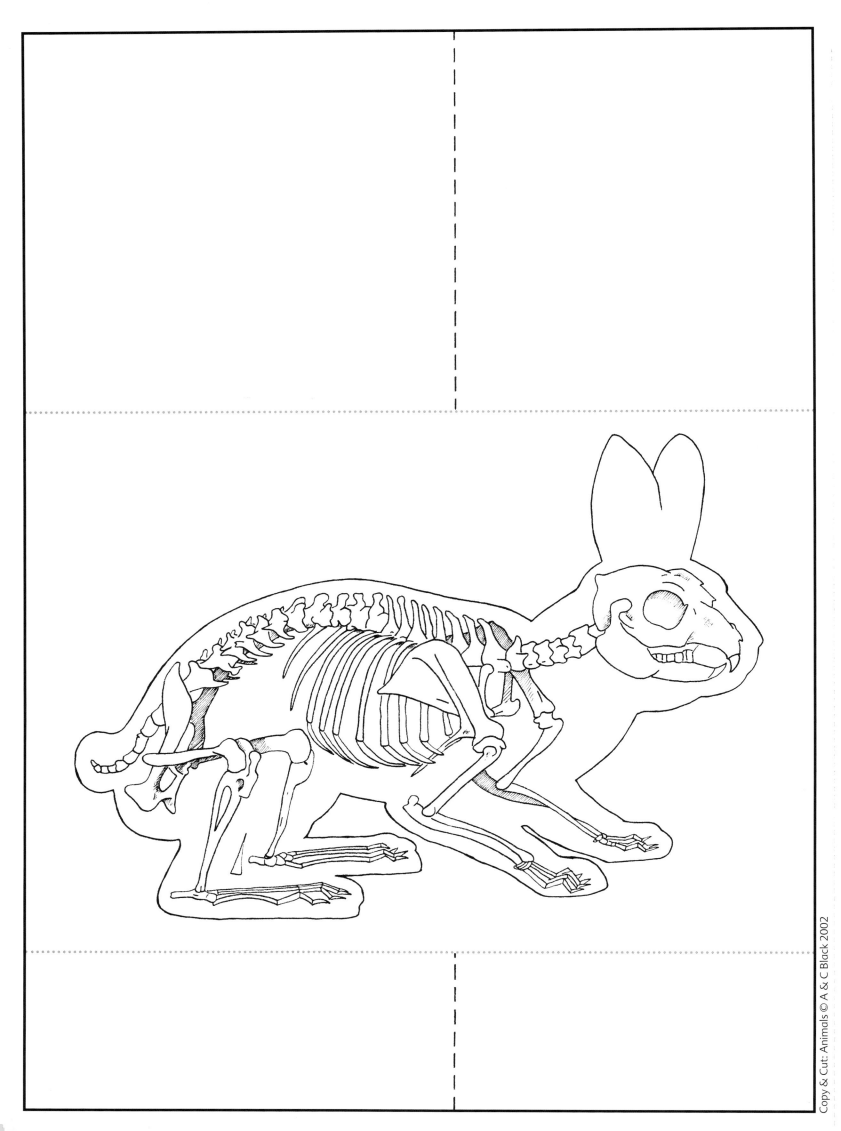

Tree visitors

Trees have lots of animal visitors. Trees provide shelter, food and a home. Many animals don't stay very long, but others spend their lives in or near a tree. Make this tree model and draw the animals you might see.

You will need: the Tree visitors template • scissors • pencil crayons for decorating

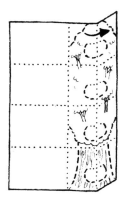

1. Fold the paper along the A dots, like this.

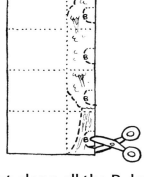

2. Cut along all the B dashes. Unfold.

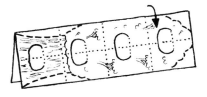

3. Fold the paper in half lengthways, like this.

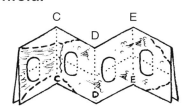

4. Fold the paper in a zig-zag along the dots (C, D, E). Start by folding forwards along the C dots.

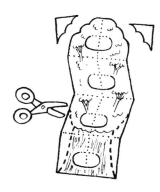

5. Unfold. Cut along the dashes to make the tree shape.

6. Fold the flaps upwards along the dots.

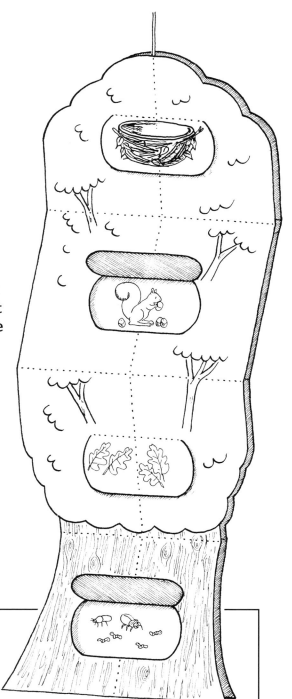

Choose a tree near your home or school. Decorate your model to look like this tree. Draw the leaf shapes and any blossom or fruit. Think about the animals you have seen on or near the tree. Draw an animal under each flap. On top of the flap, draw the part of the tree it visits or lives in.

21

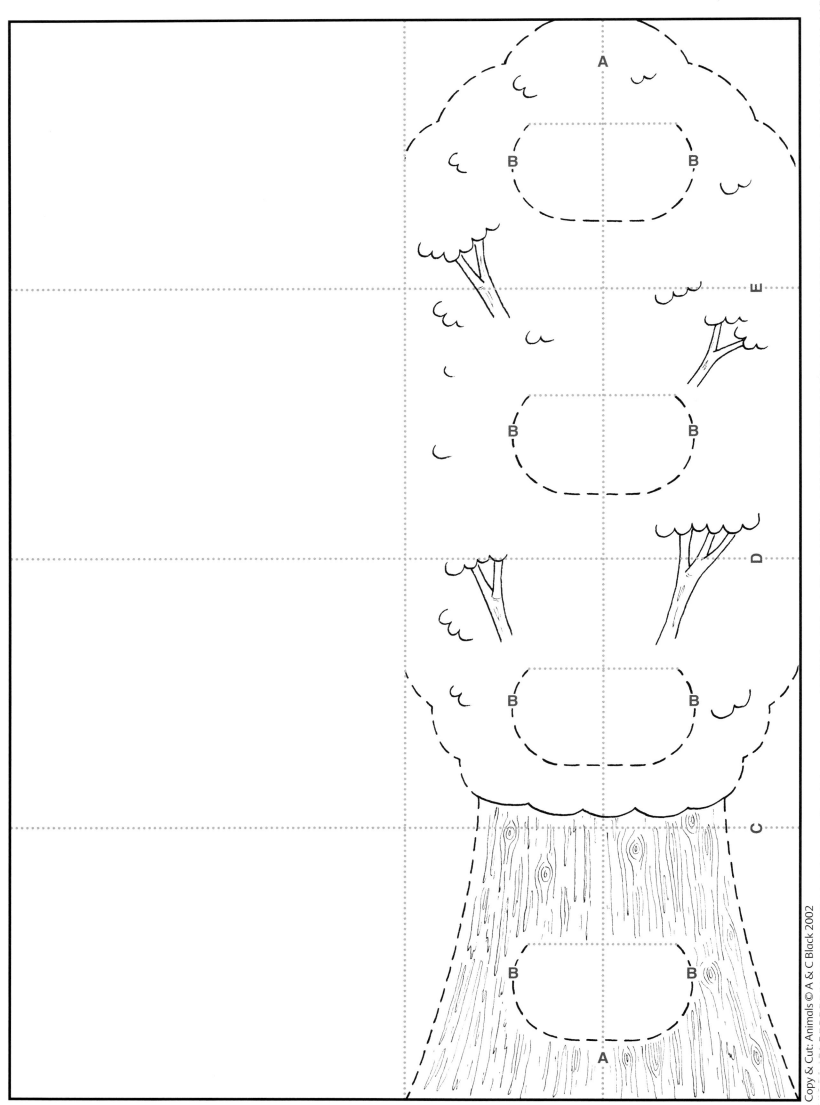

Pond scene

A pond is a perfect home for all kinds of animals! Some animals spend all their time underwater. Others visit ponds from time to time, to lay their eggs or to feed. What animals might you see in or around a pond?
Draw and label them on this scene.

You will need: the Pond scene template • scissors • pencil • pencil crayons for decorating

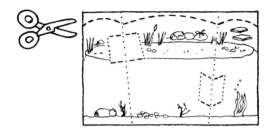

1. Cut along the A dashes.

2. Fold the paper backwards along all the B dots.

3. Cut along all the dashes.

4. Fold forwards along all the C dots. Then fold backwards. Unfold.

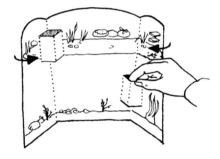

5. Unfold the paper. Fold forwards along all the B dots. Carefully pull the pop-up shapes forwards.

Press the paper flat again. Draw pond animals on the pop-up shapes and label them. Draw more animals in the pond, on the surface and around the edges. Label them too. Draw the plants that the animals might feed on.

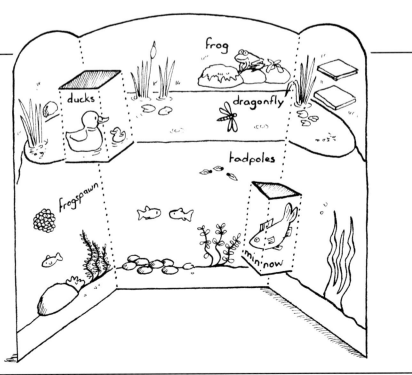

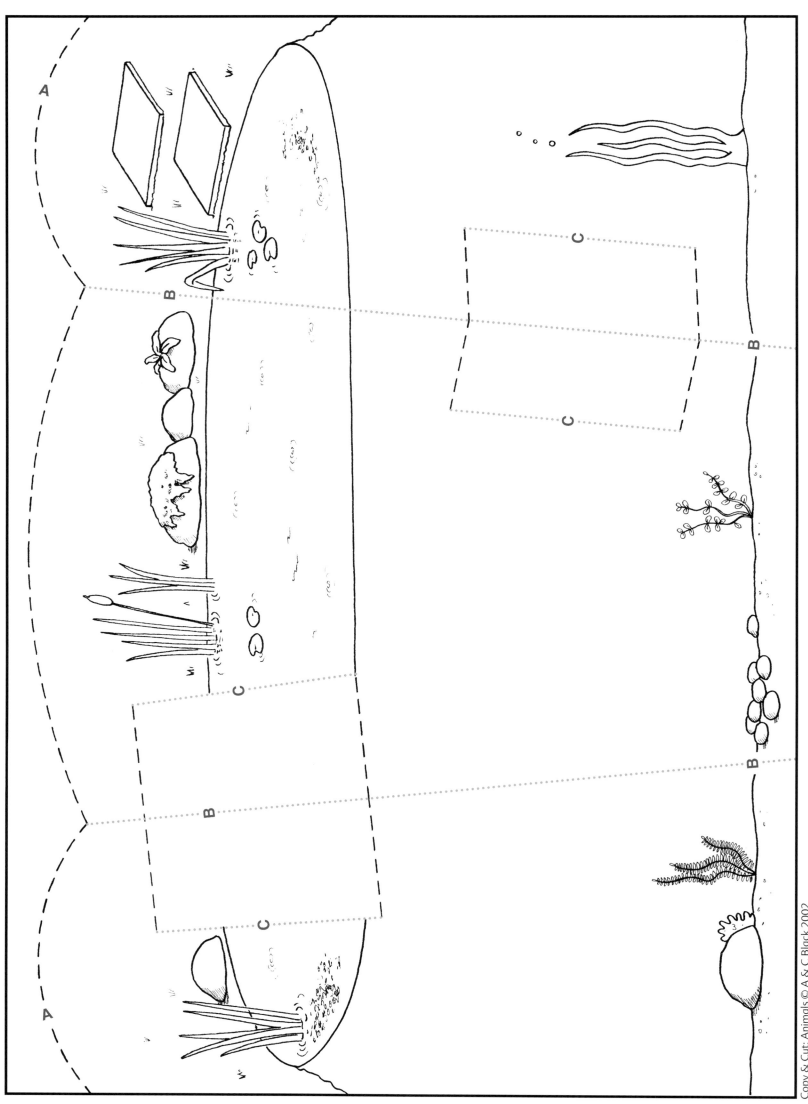

Animal notebook

You can learn a lot about animals by watching them carefully. Choose an animal to watch. It could be a pet, a farm animal or an animal kept in school.
What does the animal look like? What does it do?
Write all your notes in this book.

You will need: the Animal notebook template • scissors • glue • pencil

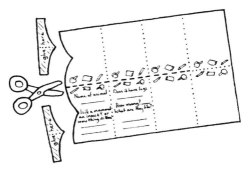

1. Cut along all the dashes. Put the two small pieces to one side.

2. Fold the paper in half lengthways, like this.

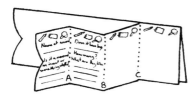

3. Fold the top piece of paper in a zig-zag along the dots (A, B, C). Start by folding forwards along the A dots.

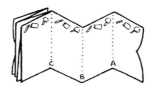

4. Turn the paper over. Do the same on the other side.

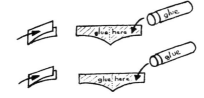

5. Fold the small pieces in half along the dots. Unfold. Spread glue where marked.

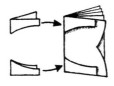

6. Wrap them around the top and bottom of your book, like this. Press down firmly.

Write a title on the cover of your book. Fill in pages 1 and 2. Think up some more questions and write one on each blank page. You could write about what the animal's body is like, how it moves, how it feeds and what it eats. Watch your animal and make notes. You could draw your animal and label the parts of its body.

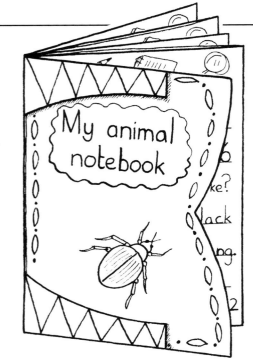

How to
look after wildlife

by _____

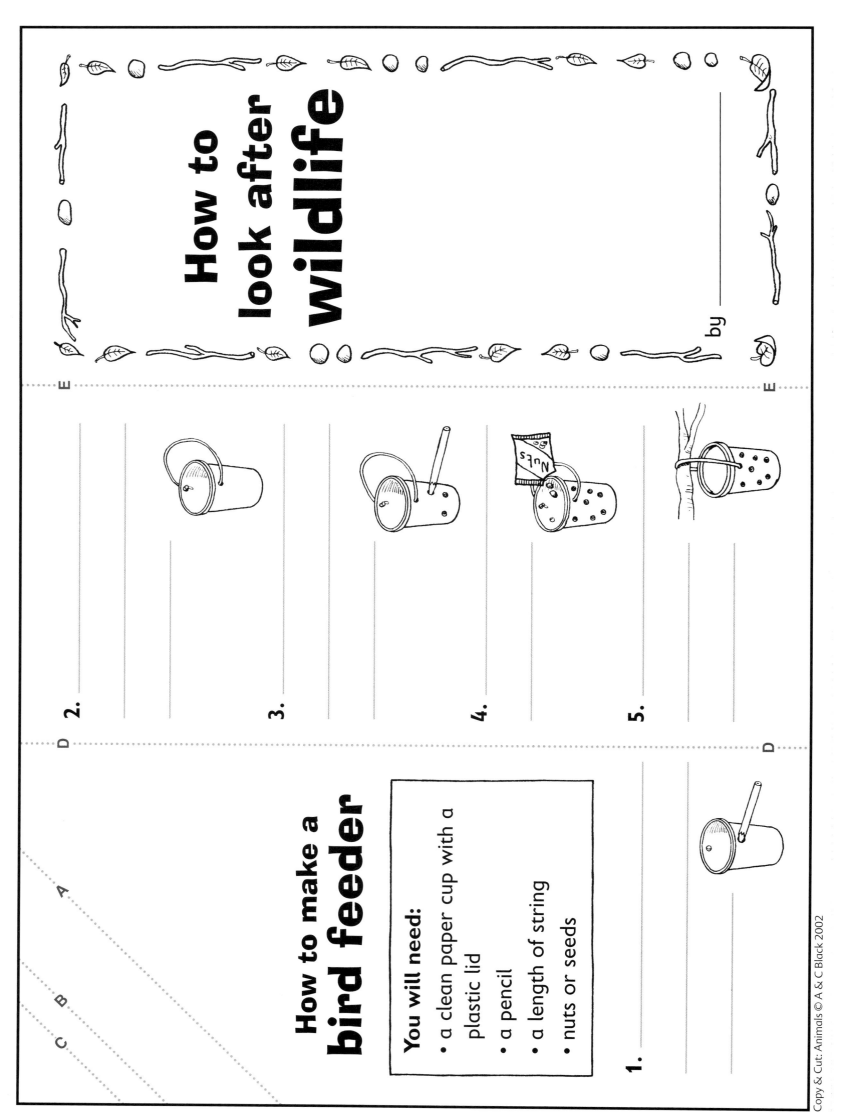

2. _____

3. _____

4. _____

5. _____

How to make a
bird feeder

You will need:

- a clean paper cup with a plastic lid
- a pencil
- a length of string
- nuts or seeds

1. _____

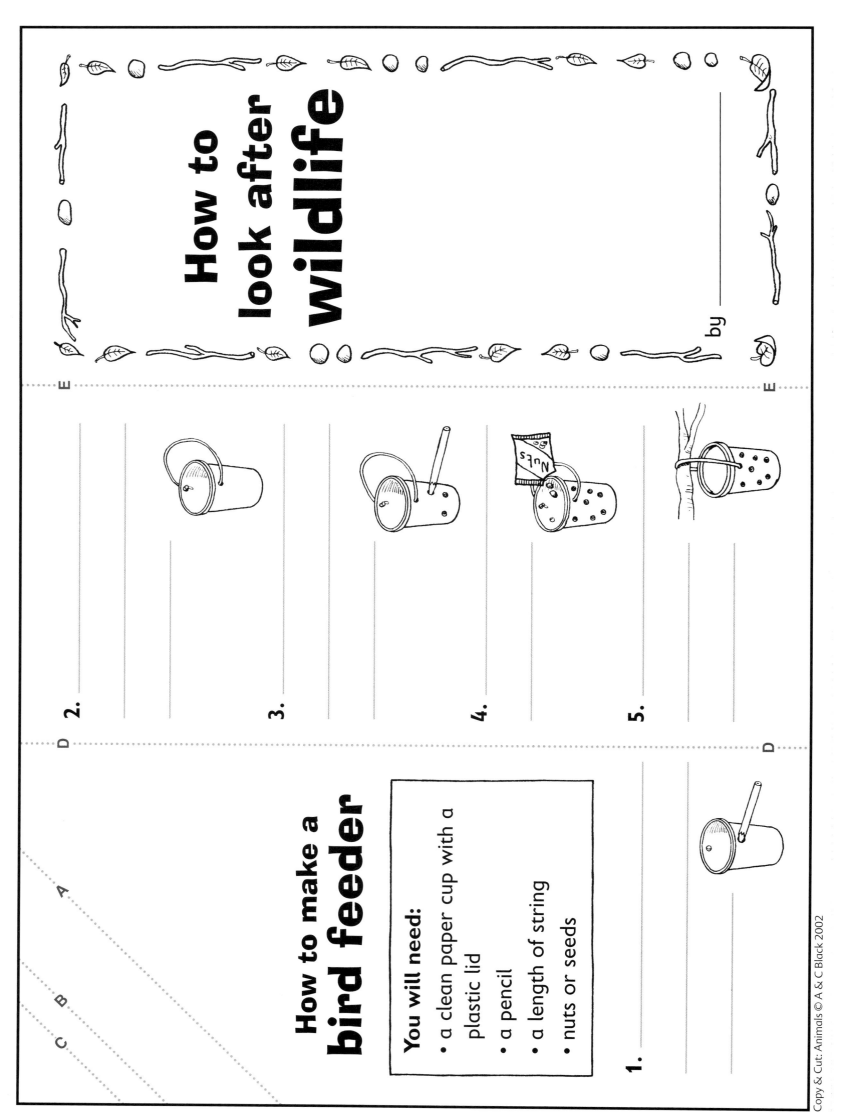

Day and night wheel

Some animals spend all day asleep and hunt for food at night! They have big eyes to help them see in the dark. Other animals are awake in the daytime and sleep during the night, the same as you. Make this wheel to show both types of animals and how they live.

You will need: the Day and night wheel template • scissors • pencil • pencil crayons for decorating

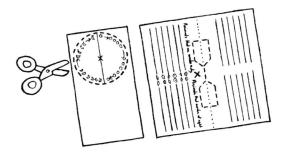  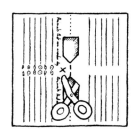

1. Cut along the A dashes. Then cut out the wheel. Put it to one side.

2. Fold the paper in half along the B dots. Cut along the dashes.

3. Open out the paper. Cut along the rest of the dashes. Then fold the paper in half again.

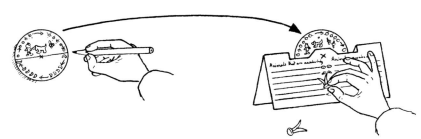

4. Draw on the wheel. Place it inside the folded paper and line up the crosses.

5. Carefully push a split pin through the two crosses. Open out the pin on the back.

Think of animals to draw on the wheel. On the half with the sun pictures, draw animals that are awake in the day. On the half with the moon pictures, draw animals that are awake at night. Then turn the wheel to change between day and night!

Write about some of the animals beneath the wheel. You could explain what they eat, and how they hunt or feed. Continue writing on the back.

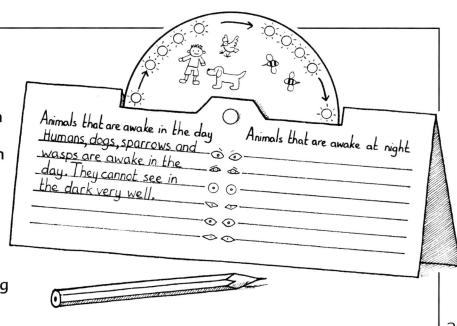

Animals that are awake in the day
Humans, dogs, sparrows and wasps are awake in the day. They cannot see in the dark very well.

Animals that are awake at night

B

Animals that are awake in the day

Animals that are awake at night

×

A --- A

Who lives here?

Look around your school grounds to see what animals you can find. Look in hidden places such as a crack in a wall, under a stone or in a bush. You might be surprised how many animals are hiding there! Use this book to show the animals and where you found them.

You will need: the Who lives here? template • scissors • pencil • pencil crayons for decorating

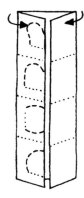

1. Start with the blank side facing you. Then fold the paper forwards along the A dots, like this.

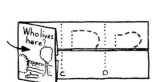
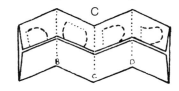

2. Fold the paper in a zig-zag along the dots (B, C, D). Start by folding forwards along the B dots.

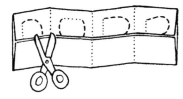

3. Cut along all the dashes.

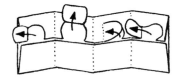

4. Fold all the flaps along the dots.

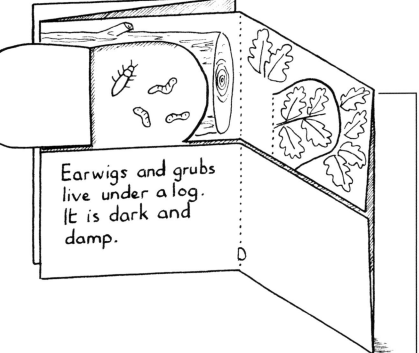

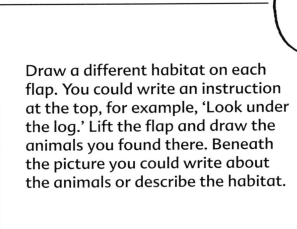

Draw a different habitat on each flap. You could write an instruction at the top, for example, 'Look under the log.' Lift the flap and draw the animals you found there. Beneath the picture you could write about the animals or describe the habitat.

Earwigs and grubs live under a log. It is dark and damp.

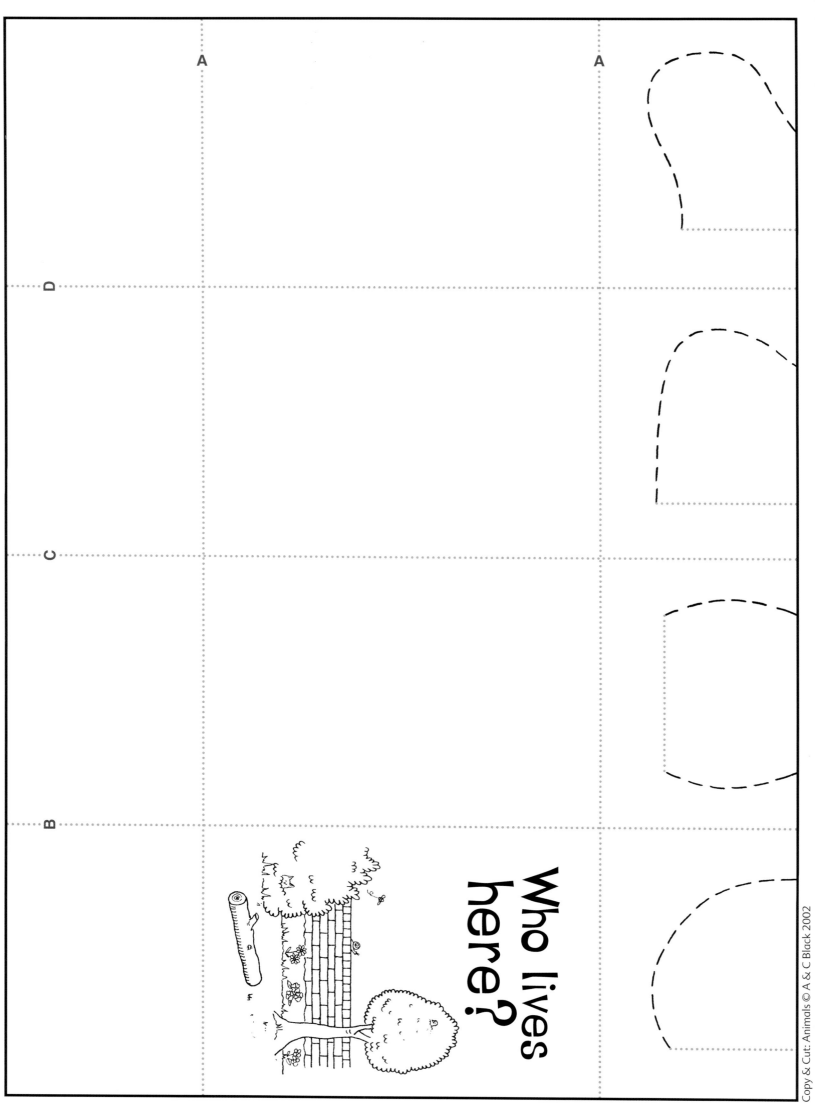

Who lives here?

Overground, underground

Many animals make their homes underground, where it is warm and dry. There, they can hide from other animals that want to eat them. An underground den is also a safe place for baby animals to grow up. Show animals that live above and below the ground on this model.

You will need: the Overground, underground template • scissors • pencil • pencil crayons for decorating

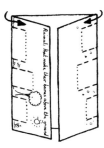

1. Start with the blank side facing you. Then fold the paper forwards along the A dots, like this.

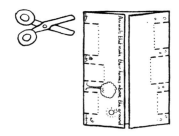
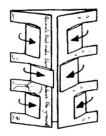

2. Cut along all the dashes.

3. Fold all the flaps forwards along the dots. Then fold backwards. Unfold.

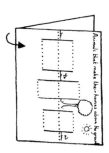

4. Open out the paper. Fold it in half widthways, like this.

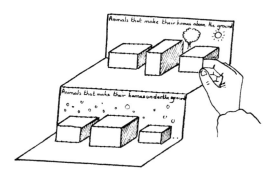

5. Fold forwards along all the A dots. Then pull the pop-up shapes forwards.

Press the paper flat again. Use information books to find pictures of animals that make their homes above and below the ground. Draw the animals on the pop-up shapes. Write a label or caption for each animal. Then colour the backgrounds.

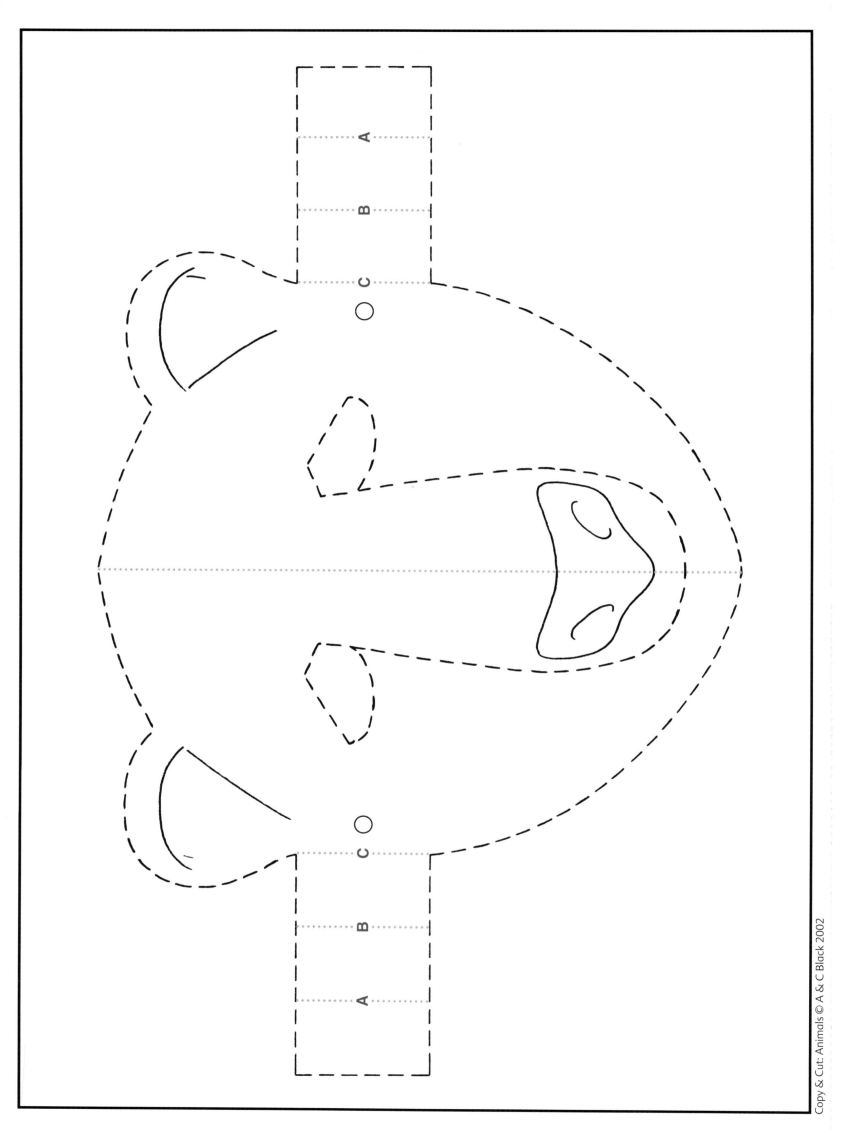

A

B

C

C

B

A

Leopard mask

This mask will turn you into a leopard! Leopards live in forests and grasslands in Africa and Asia. You are going to imagine that you are a leopard. Put on this mask and tell your friends all about your life as a fierce hunter.

You will need: the Leopard mask template • scissors • hole puncher • a length of elastic • pencil crayons, yellow and black paper and glue for decorating

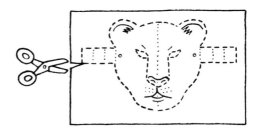

1. Cut along the dashes around the edge of the mask.

2. Fold the mask in half along the dots. Cut along the dashes around the nose and eyes. Unfold.

3. Fold the side flaps in a zig-zag along the dots (A, B, C). Start by folding backwards along the A dots.

4. Use a hole puncher to make holes in the circles.

5. Cut a length of elastic to fit your head. Tie it through the holes.

Decorate your mask by gluing on pieces of yellow and black paper. Then make notes about leopards, using information books and CD-ROMs to help you.

Put on your mask and become a leopard. Explain to a friend how you live. Say what you do during the day, what you eat and how you hunt.

37

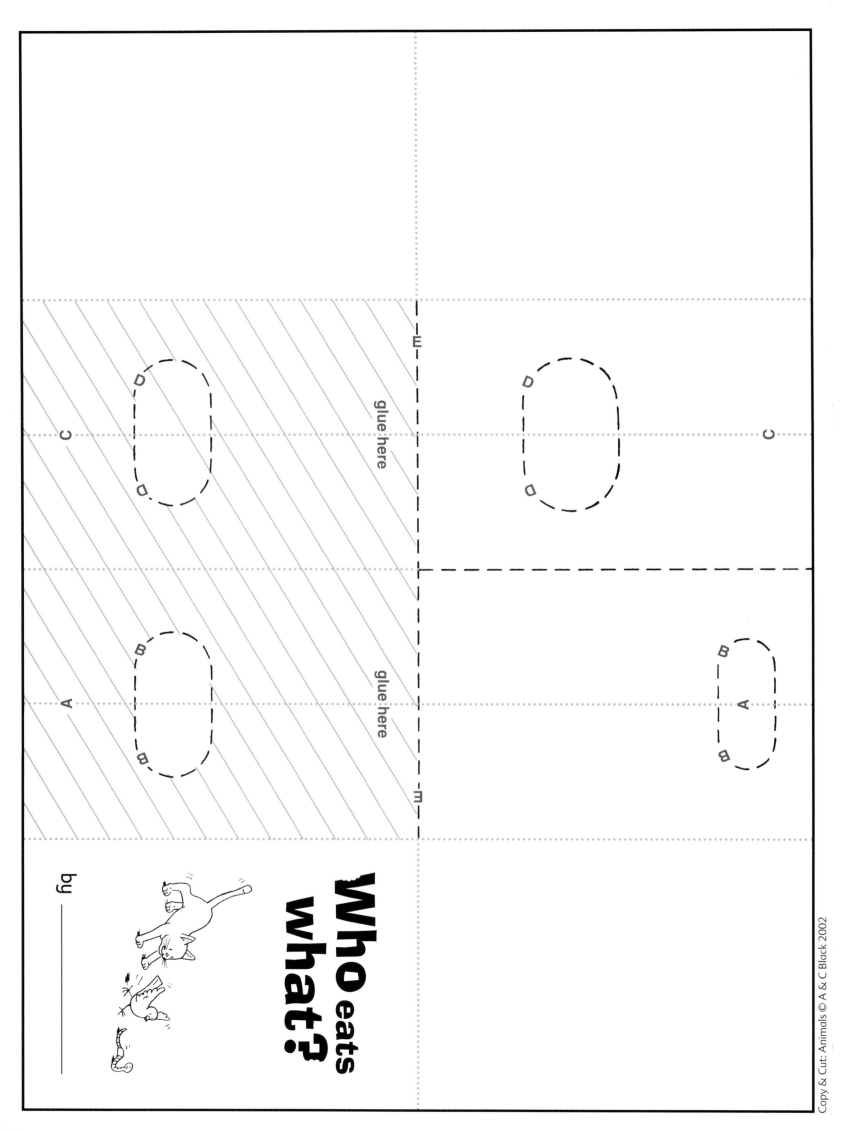

glue here

glue here

E

C

C

D

D

B

A

B

A

Who eats what?

by _____

All about ladybirds

What do you know about ladybirds? Think about what colours they are, how they move around and where you might see them. Make this card and decorate it to look just like a ladybird. You can write about ladybirds inside the wings.

You will need: the All about ladybirds template • scissors • pencil • pencil crayons, red and black paper, red sweet wrappers and glue for decorating

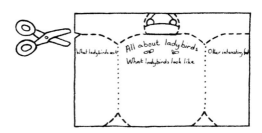

1. Cut along all the dashes.

2. Fold the paper forwards along the dots.

Open the wings again and write about ladybirds inside. Use information books to help you.

Then close the wings. Look at pictures of ladybirds and decorate the outside of the card. You could glue on red paper or sweet wrappers. Use circles of black paper for spots. You could also make legs and antennae from black paper.

B

by ————

My pop-up
bee book

C C

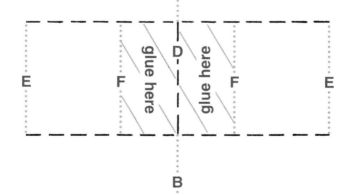

E ⋮ F | glue here | D | glue here | F ⋮ E

B

A — — — — — — — — — — — — — — — — — — A

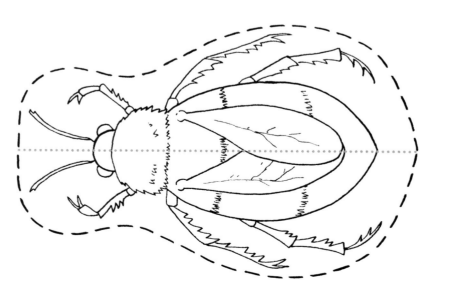

I spy an animal

Choose a place near your home or school, such as a park, your garden, your yard or waste ground. On this pop-up scene, you can draw the place and show all the animals that live there. Challenge a friend to find all the animals hiding in your scene!

You will need: the I spy an animal template • scissors • pencil • pencil crayons for decorating

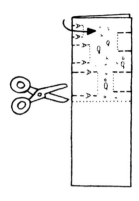

1. Fold the paper in half lengthways, like this. Cut along all the A dashes.

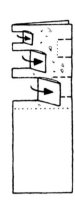

2. Fold the flaps forwards along the B dots. Then fold backwards. Unfold.

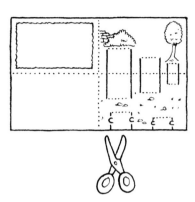

3. Open out the paper. Cut along the C dashes.

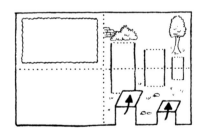

4. Fold the flaps along the D dots. Unfold.

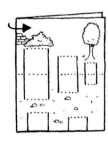

5. Fold the paper in half widthways, like this.

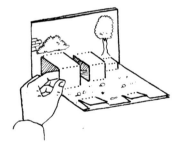

6. Fold the paper in half again. Then pull the pop-up shapes forwards.

Press your scene flat again. Decorate it to show the place you have chosen. Draw the habitats you saw, such as bushes, stones or flower-beds. Draw animals in the scene and hiding under the flaps. Write a title and draw a picture on the front cover.

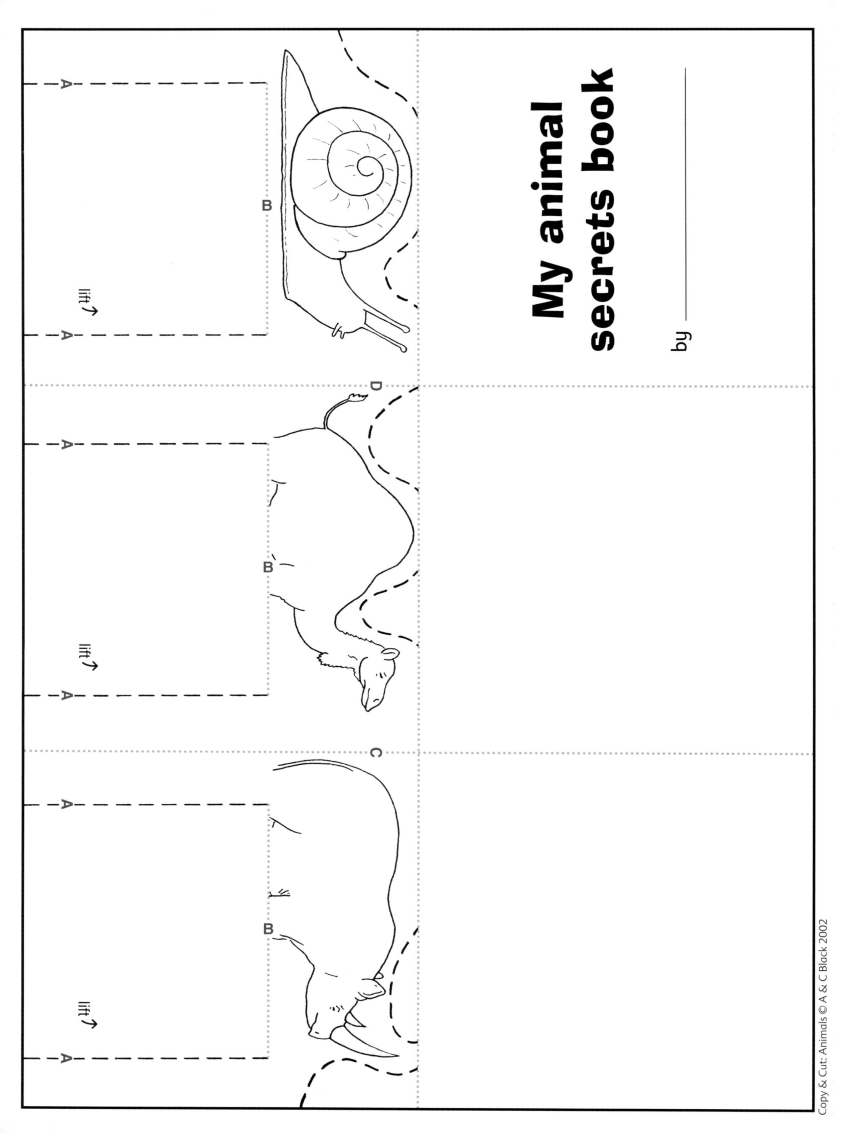

My animal secrets book

by _____

A → ← lift A →

B

A → ← lift A →

D

B

A → ← lift A →

C

B

Once I saw...

You are going to create your own animal! Think up an animal that no one has ever seen. What does it looks like? It might have soft fur or dry, scaly skin. Perhaps it has sharp teeth or a spiky tail? Make this model and turn it into your animal.

You will need: the Once I saw... template • scissors • pencil • pencil crayons, coloured paper and fabric for decorating

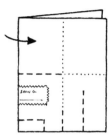

1. Fold the paper in half widthways, like this.

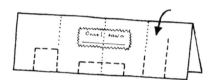

2. Cut along the A dashes. Unfold.

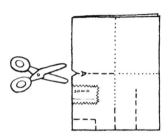

3. Fold the paper in half lengthways, like this.

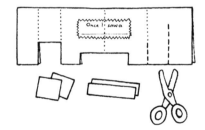

4. Cut along all the dashes.

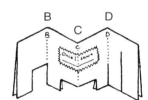

5. Fold the paper in a zig-zag along the dots (B, C, D). Start by folding forwards along the B dots.

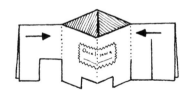

6. Unfold. Push the left and right edges towards each other, so that you make a box shape in the middle.

Press your model flat again. Cut out shapes along the edges to make it look like your made-up animal. You could cut triangles to make spikes or cut wavy lines to make humps. Make sure it can still stand up! Now decorate your animal. Use coloured pencils or glue on pieces of paper and fabric. Write its name in the box.

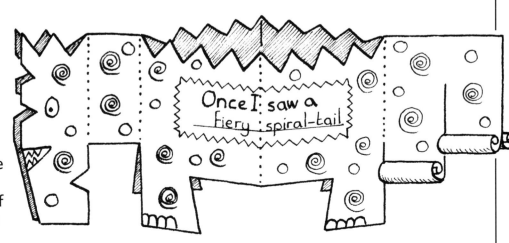

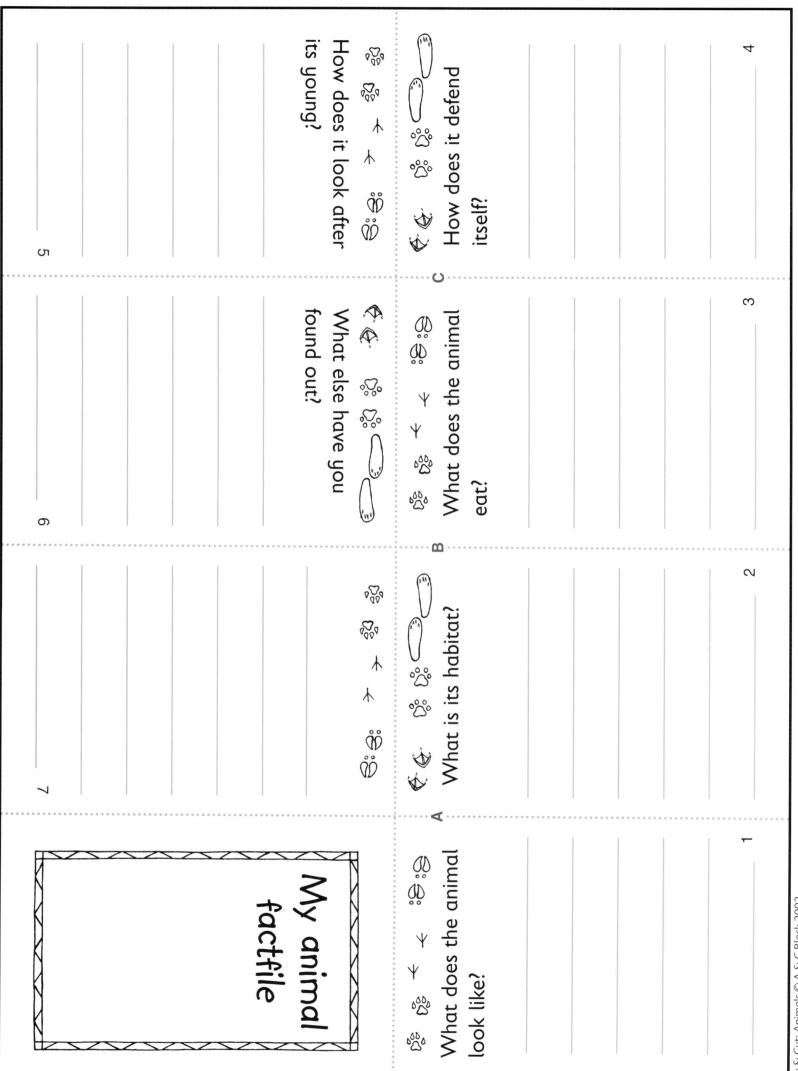

4

C How does it defend itself?

How does it look after its young?

5

3

B What does the animal eat?

What else have you found out?

6

2

A What is its habitat?

7

1

What does the animal look like?

My animal factfile

Quiz book

Choose an animal and use this quiz book to test how much your friends know about it. Remember that when you write a quiz, you need to know all the answers yourself! Write your questions in the book. Pull the strips to hide or show the answers.

You will need: the Quiz book template • scissors • pencil • scrap paper • pencil crayons for decorating

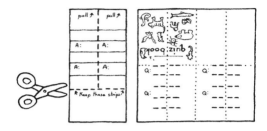 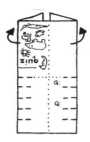 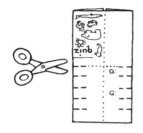

1. Cut along all the A dashes. Put the two long strips to one side.

2. Fold the paper backwards along the B dots.

3. Cut along all the dashes. Unfold.

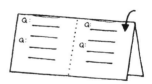 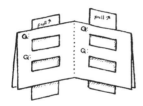

4. Fold the paper in half along the C dots.

5. Fold it in half again to make a book. Unfold.

6. Slot the strips into the top of the book. Slide them through the slots in an over, under pattern.

Write four questions about the animal on a piece of scrap paper. Check the answers in an information book and write them down. Then write the questions in your book. Draw pictures in the empty boxes on the strips.

Now pull the strips up and write the answers. Push the strips back down to hide the answers. Write your name on the front cover. Give your book to a friend to try out your quiz!

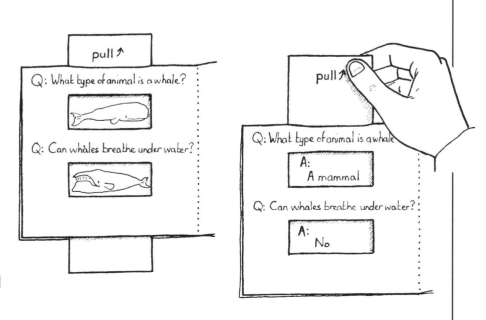

quiz book

___'s

pull ↑

pull ↑

A:

A:

A:

A:

Q:

Q:

Q:

Q:

↑ Keep these strips. ↑

Research file

Scientists spend lots of time doing research to find out more about animals. You can do your own animal research with this handy file. Plan which books, CD-ROMs and websites you will use. Write down all the useful information you find out.

You will need: the Research file template • scissors • pencil • pencil crayons for decorating

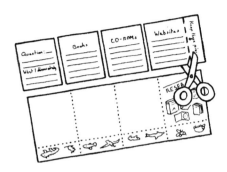 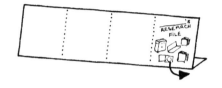

1. Cut along all the A dashes. Put the four small pieces of paper to one side.

2. Fold the paper backwards along the B dots.

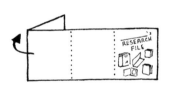 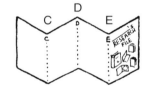 

3. Fold the paper in a zig-zag along the dots (C, D, E). Start by folding backwards along the C dots.

4. Slot the four pieces of paper into your research file to make the pages.

Take the pages out of the file. On the first page, write a question that you would like to research. Write what you know already. On the other pages, plan where you will look to find out the answer. Write the title and author of each book or CD-ROM. Write the address of each website.

Then research the answer. Write on the backs of the pages and make extra pages from scrap paper if you need to. Note down all the useful information and write where you found it.

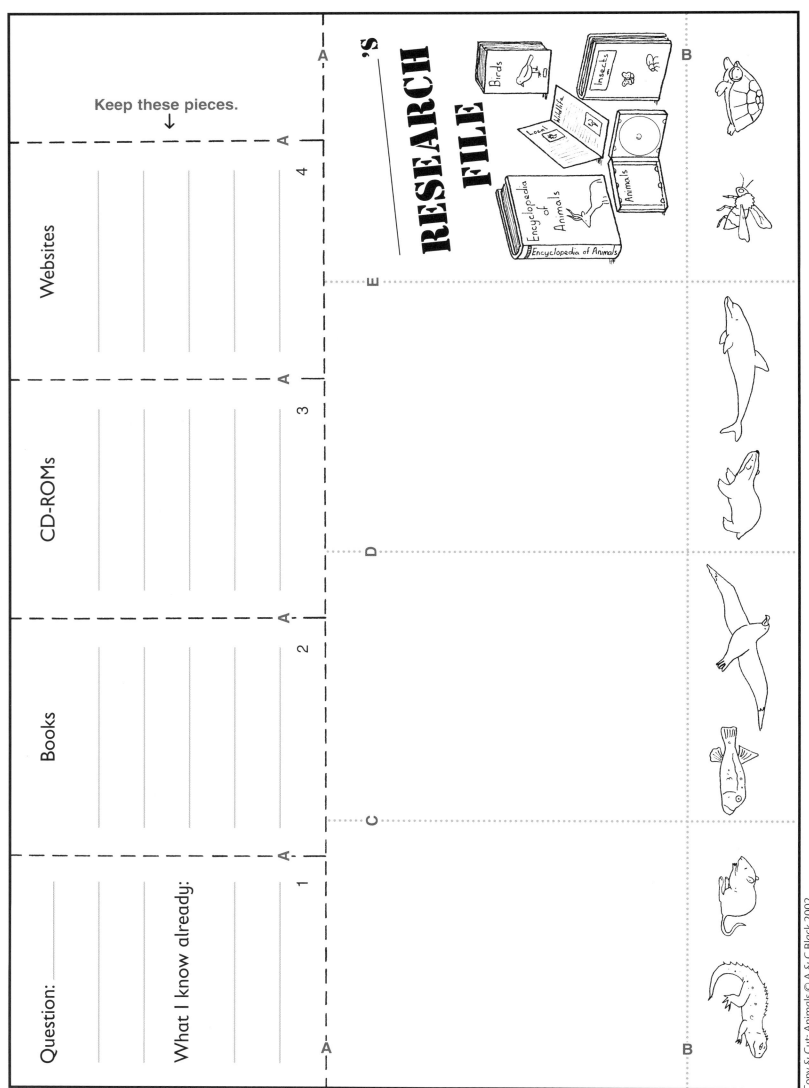

Question:

What I know already:

Books

CD-ROMs

Websites

Keep these pieces.

RESEARCH FILE

'S

Encyclopedia of Animals

Birds

Insects

Wildlife

Local

Animals

Glossary of animal parts

A glossary is usually at the back of an information book. People use the glossary to look up words they don't understand. The words are in alphabetical order so that it is easy to find them. In this book you can write your own glossary of words for animal parts.

You will need: the Glossary of animal parts template • scissors • pencil • pencil crayons for decorating

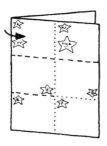

1. Fold the paper in half widthways, like this. Unfold.

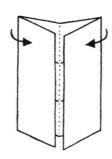

2. Fold the paper forwards along the A dots. Unfold.

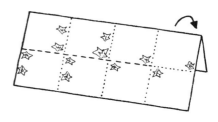

3. Fold the paper backwards along the B dots and dashes. Unfold.

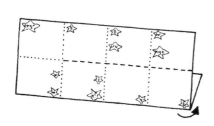

4. Fold the paper backwards along the C dots and dashes. Unfold.

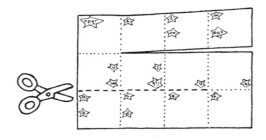

5. Cut along all the dashes.

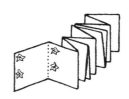

6. Fold the paper in a zig-zag along the dots.

Make a list of words for animal parts. Write them in alphabetical order in your glossary. Use the letters on the pages to help you. Next to each word, write a short definition to help someone who doesn't know what the word means. Use information books if you need to. Remember to write a title and your name on the front cover.

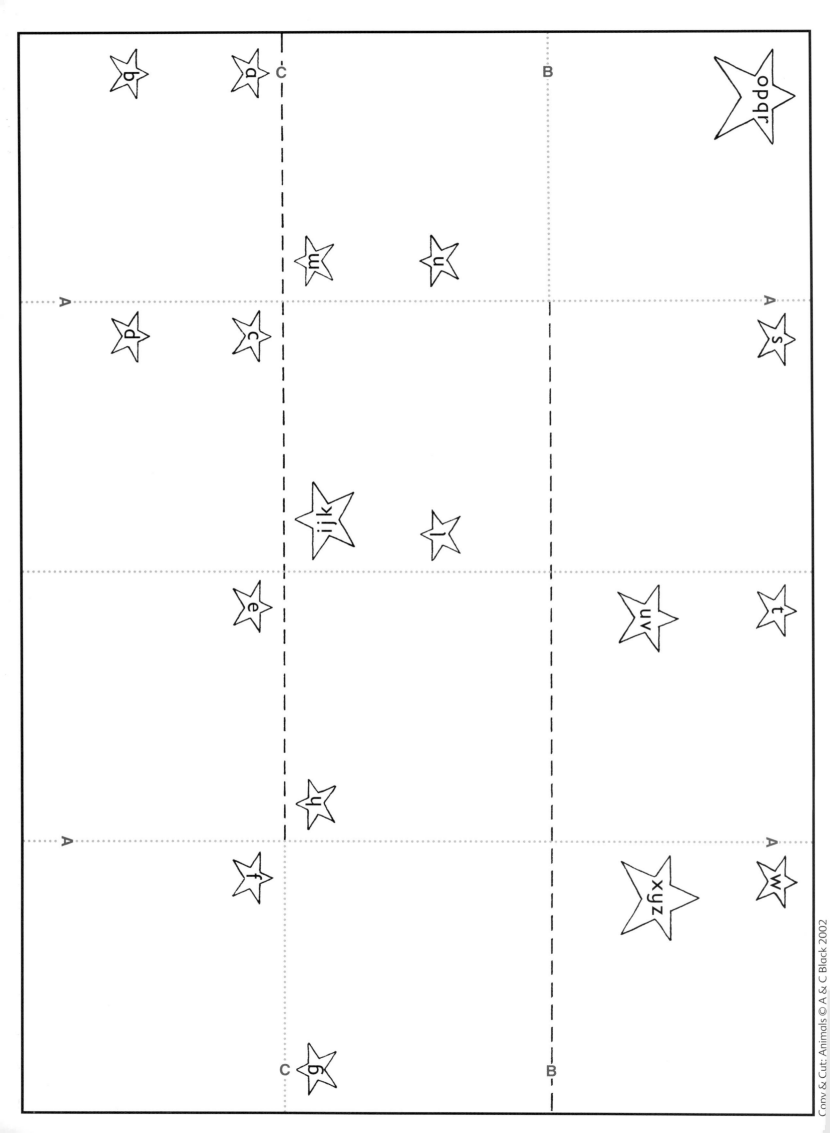

Helpful hints

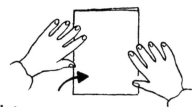

Fold along the **dots**

Cut along the **dashes**

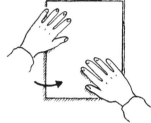

fold **widthways**

fold **lengthways**

fold **forwards**   fold **backwards**

Zig-zag
Fold forwards along the first dotted line.
Fold backwards along the second dotted line.
Fold forwards along the third dotted line.
Continue until you reach the end.

This is the
left edge

This is the
right edge

Using scissors

 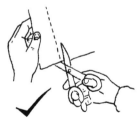

Do not put your hand holding the paper in front of the scissors.

Close the scissors when you are not using them.

Make sure the scissors don't get hidden under pieces of paper.

Drawing mammals

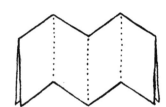

Start by drawing a body shape. Then change it a little, to look like the animal you want to draw.

Draw the neck and head on one side of the body. Use pictures of animals to help you.

Then draw the legs. They might be short, long, thick or thin. Draw other parts such as the tail.

59

Teachers' notes

by Christine Moorcroft

Mammal misfits (pages 5–6)

Science unit: 2C Variation — *Recognising that living things can be grouped according to similarities and differences*

Introduce the project by talking about mammals. You will need a large picture of a mammal (side view), fixed on to a display board and covered. You will also need other pictures of animals, including mammals and non-mammals. Show the children a picture of an animal. Ask them if it is a mammal and how they can tell. Write their responses on the board. Discuss whether or not they are right. (A mammal has a backbone and is warm-blooded. Young mammals drink their mothers' milk. Most mammals have hair or fur and give birth to live young.) Repeat this procedure for several animals. Then tell the children that you have a picture of a mystery animal which you will uncover a little at a time for them to guess what it is. Uncover the back section first. Ask the children what mammal they think it is and what clues they can see. Continue, revealing the middle section and then the front of the animal.

Provide pictures of mammals for the children to copy in their books. Encourage them to choose mammals with distinctive features. Show them how to line up the animals' body parts by drawing one section at a time and using the rhino and moose illustrations as guides for where to draw.

True or false? (pages 7–8)

Science unit: 2C Variation — *Observing simple characteristics of animals*

Begin with a statement about a type of animal, such as 'All birds can fly.' Ask the children to give evidence which shows this might be true: for example, a blackbird can fly, an eagle can fly and a parrot can fly. Explain that even though there are many examples which suggest that the statement is true, it may still not be true. Ask if they can think of any evidence which proves the statement false (for example, ostriches and penguins cannot fly). Help the children to write questions which they will be able to answer using information books and CD-ROMs in the classroom. After they have completed their projects, the children could contribute to a display of 'true' statements. Encourage others to share any evidence they have found which proves statements not to be true.

Riddle book (pages 9–10)

Science unit: 2C Variation — *Observing simple characteristics of animals*
Literacy objectives: Y2 T3 T8, 11 *Riddles*

Before beginning the project, read examples of riddles to the children and help them to work out the answers. Encourage them to think of several possible answers for each riddle and then choose the one that is the best match. Ensure that reference books are readily available so that the children can check the information they use in their riddles.

Fantastic fish (pages 11–12)

Science unit: 2C Variation — *Observing simple characteristics of animals*
Literacy objectives: Y1 T1 W12 • Y1 T2 W10 • Y1 T3 W8 • Y2 T1 W10 • Y2 T2 W10 • Y2 T3 W9 *Vocabulary extension*

Provide illustrated information books about fish, and leaflets from fishmongers and tropical fish dealers (or printouts from related websites). Discuss the fish, for example, whether they are long or short, narrow or wide, and the number and position of the fins. You could introduce terms such as 'tail fin' and 'dorsal fin'.

The children could use a chart to record which fish have bright colours and which have dull colours:

Brightly coloured fish	Dull-coloured fish
angel fish	plaice

Discuss the ways in which colour is used in nature: some animals have patterns and colours which blend in with their surroundings. This is so that other animals, hunting for food, cannot see them easily. Others have bright colours which might signal a warning that they are poisonous.

Ocean creatures (pages 13–14)

Science unit: 2C Variation — *Observing simple characteristics of animals*

Provide illustrated information books about sea animals, and leaflets from retailers about the fish and seafoods they sell. Reinforce the wide variety of creatures that live in the ocean. Help the children to formulate questions about the animals which will develop their understanding of why they prefer certain habitats: for example, 'Does the animal need to come out of the water sometimes? What for?', 'What does it eat?', 'How does it feed?' and 'What eats it?' The template could be enlarged to A3 so that several children can contribute to one model.

Growing up (pages 15–16)

Science unit: 2A Health and growth — *Recognising that animals produce young and these grow into new adults*

Copy the template on to A3 paper if possible. Begin the lesson by showing a video or a series of photographs of the different stages in a frog's life. Ask the children to notice the ways in which the frog changes, including shape and size and the growth or loss of features such as a tail, suckers and legs. Introduce the words 'egg', 'tadpole', 'froglet' and 'frog' and write them on the board. Explain that the life cycle is continuous, from egg to adult and then beginning again with new eggs. After completing the project, the children could find out about the ways in which some adult animals look after their young or provide for it to survive alone. The template could be adapted to depict the life cycle of a different animal such as a butterfly or dragonfly.

Snake mobile (pages 17–18)

Science unit: 2C Variation — *Observing simple characteristics of animals*
Literacy objectives: Y1 T1 W10 • Y1 T2 W7 *Critical features of words*

You could copy this template on to card so that the mobile holds its shape well (alternatively collaging the snake will have the same effect). Introduce the project by writing the word 'snake' on the board. Ask what it makes the children think of and whether they like snakes (and why or why not). Record their responses. Talk about the reasons why many people dislike snakes or are frightened of them.

Encourage the class to share ideas for the poem and discuss the ways in which snakes are similar to, and different from, other familiar animals. The children could list the ways in which a snake is different from a dog:

Snake	Dog
no legs rough, scaly skin long, forked tongue lays eggs	four legs furry skin smooth, rounded tongue has live young

What's inside? (pages 19–20)

Science unit: 1A Ourselves
Literacy objectives: Y1 T1 W12 • Y1 T2 W10 • Y1 T3 W8 • Y2 T1 W10 • Y2 T2 W10 • Y2 T3 W9 *Vocabulary extension*

To introduce the topic, ask the children to feel some of their own bones. Ask where they have bones. Tell them the names of bones such as arm bones, leg bones, ribs, skull, backbone (or spine), shoulder blade, collarbone and hip bone. You could show them a labelled picture of a human skeleton. Talk about the purpose of bones. Some bones protect the parts inside them, such as the skull which protects the brain and the ribs which protect the heart and lungs.

Look at the rabbit skeleton on the template and invite the children to compare it with a human skeleton. Discuss how a skeleton reflects the way an animal moves. To follow up the project, ask the children to pretend they have no skeleton during PE lessons. Invite them to describe what their bodies would be like.

Tree visitors (pages 21–22)

Science unit: 2B Plants and animals in the local environment

Choose a tree for the children to observe before they make the project. Groups could observe the same tree in the school grounds at different times, or the whole class could observe different trees in a park. Help the children to identify the type of tree by its shape, leaves, bark and any flowers or seeds they can see on it. Encourage the children to look for animals — on the bark, on the leaves, under the leaves, on the ground near the tree and in the air around it. Help them to describe and then identify anything they find. Useful questions to aid identification include: 'Does it have legs? How many?' 'Does it have wings?' 'What colour is it?' 'What patterns can you see on it?' 'How does it move?' 'What is it doing?' Encourage the children to make notes about each animal and the tree itself, to use when completing the project.

Pond scene (pages 23–24)

Science unit: 2B Plants and animals in the local environment

If possible, take the children pond-dipping before they begin the project. It is important first to check the school's health and safety procedures for such work. Useful pond-dipping equipment includes: a plastic sieve (much easier to handle than a long-handled net), shallow white containers such as pie dishes and — if the children are going to study any animals for a short time in school — plastic pots with lids. Show the children how to drag the sieve through the water, then tip it upside down over a container containing pond water. Provide illustrated information books about pond animals for the children to look at when decorating their projects.

Animal notebook (pages 25–26)

Science unit: 2C Variation — *Observing simple characteristics of animals*
Literacy objectives: Y1 T3 T21 • Y2 T3 T21 • Y3 T1 T23 *Writing non-chronological reports*

Introduce the topic by talking about familiar animals such as pets. Ask what the children have learnt about the animals by watching them. You could arrange for the children to observe an animal kept in school. Provide information books or definitions to help them decide what kind of animal it is (a mammal, an insect and so on). Demonstrate how to write questions about the animal, starting with general ones and then moving on to more focused ones. Ask the children to think about how the animal reacts to things it hears and sees, as well as what it looks like. The children could use their notes to help them write a non-chronological report. As an extension activity, they could contribute to a chart on which they record something an animal did, what happened which seemed to cause this, and why they think the animal behaves in this way:

Animal	What it did	What happened to make it do this	Why it might do this
cat	purred	someone stroked its back	it likes being stroked

Wildlife leaflet (pages 27–28)

Science unit: 2B Plants and animals in the local environment
Literacy objectives: Y1 T1 T16 • Y2 T1 T15 • Y3 T2 T16 *Writing instructions*

Choose a habitat as the focus of this project, for example a part of the school grounds. Discuss ideas for looking after the habitat and encouraging wildlife, such as helping plants to grow (to provide food for animals) and not dropping litter. You could give the children copies of the Countryside Code to use for ideas. Talk about how the children can encourage wildlife and help animals to survive the winter by putting out bread and milk and bird feeders. Demonstrate to the class how to make the bird feeder (using a paper cup with a plastic lid, like those provided by takeaway restaurants): 1) Use a pencil to make two holes near the top of a paper cup. 2) Push a length of string through the holes and tie knots on the inside. 3) Use a pencil to make lots of small holes in the side of the cup. 4) Put nuts or seeds in the cup. 5) Put the lid on the cup and hang it on a branch.

Day and night wheel (pages 29–30)

Science unit: 2B Plants and animals in the local environment

Ask the children what time they go to bed and get up. Discuss whether their pets sleep at different times from them. They might have cats which hunt outside at night or hamsters which sleep for most of the day and feed at night. Show the children pictures of animals which hunt at night, such as cats and owls. Talk about the eyes of these animals, which let in a great deal of light. This allows them to see when there is little natural light. Explain how bats find their way at night using a kind of radar, which helps them to sense the presence of large objects and other animals. When the children have made their wheels, they could write questions to help them to find out more about the behaviour of owls, cats and bats at night.

Who lives here? (pages 31–32)

Science unit: 2B Plants and animals in the local environment

Choose a part of the school grounds for the children to investigate for this activity (or different groups could investigate different areas so that the findings can be compared). Ask the children to look at small habitats within the larger one: for example, a bush, different sides of a wall, a flower-bed, a rotting log, a tree or a small patch of stony earth. Provide reference books to help the children identify the animals they find. After the children have recorded their findings in their books, ask them to describe the conditions in the habitat they studied: for example, was it dark or light, wet or dry, warm or cold, sheltered or exposed? Encourage them to think about why each animal might like its habitat.

In school the children could set up investigations to find out about the conditions preferred by different animals: for example, by providing 'choice chambers' for animals such as woodlice:

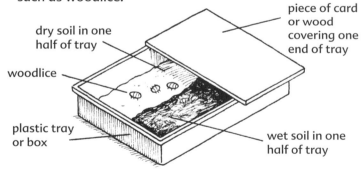

dry soil in one half of tray

piece of card or wood covering one end of tray

woodlice

plastic tray or box

wet soil in one half of tray

Overground, underground (pages 33–34)

Science unit: 2B Plants and animals in the local environment

Literacy objectives: Y1 T2 T19 • Y2 T3 T13, 14 • Y3 T1 T17 *Reading non-fiction, using non-fiction books to answer questions*

Provide reference books about animals and their homes. Before beginning, the children could observe a small patch of ground and the animals that live on or in it. They could dig up a section of the ground to look for animals in it. Help them to identify the animals they find. The same patch of ground (or another similar one) could be investigated at another time, to compare findings. Discuss which animals are found only above the ground, which are found only below it, and which can be found both above and below it. The children can record the animals they found on their models.

Polar bear mask and Leopard mask (pages 35–38)

Science unit: 2C Variation – *Observing simple characteristics of animals*

Literacy objectives: Y1 T2 T9 • Y2 T2 T7 • Y3 T1 T10 *Role-play and dialogue*

Show the children pictures of polar bears and leopards, and provide information books about them. Discuss the part of the world each animal lives in, and ask the children to think about how the environment might affect the animals. Organise the children into pairs, with one making the polar bear mask and the other the leopard mask. When they have researched the animals, they can role-play a conversation, asking questions about each other's lifestyles.

Useful information: polar bears

Polar bears live in areas in and near the Arctic Circle. A polar bear's whitish fur camouflages it against the background of ice and snow. This helps it to stalk and capture seals. It also eats fish, seaweed, grass, birds and caribou. A polar bear has a thick, water-repellent coat, which helps it to survive in icy water. It can swim for long distances. The bear's feet are broad: this helps it to move across ice. It has hair on the soles of its feet to insulate them from the cold.

Useful information: leopards

A leopard is a big cat related to the lion and tiger. Leopards are found in nearly all of Africa south of the Sahara, and also in northeast Africa and parts of Asia including India and China. A leopard's coat is yellowish above and white below, with dark spots in arranged in rosettes over most of its body. This pattern helps to camouflage the animal as it lies in the shade of trees or moves through long grass. A leopard hunts alone in the bush and forest — mainly at night when the air is cooler, although it may also bask in the sunshine. It feeds on animals such as antelopes and deer. A leopard is a good swimmer and can climb trees; it often stores the remains of animals it has killed in the branches of a tree to keep them safe.

Who eats what? (pages 39–40)

Science units: 2A Health and growth • 3A Teeth and eating

Introduce the topic by discussing what familiar animals eat. Talk about different kinds of birds and what they feed on: for example, mice, fish, worms, snails or seeds. Put together a short food chain by choosing an animal that a bird might eat, such as a snail, and asking what that animal feeds on (plants). Discuss the fact that plants make their own food. Show the children how to form a simple food chain, for example:

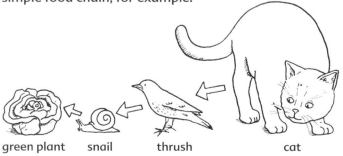

green plant   snail   thrush   cat

Provide information books so that the children can find out what familiar animals eat and make their own simple food chains.

All about ladybirds (pages 41–42)

Science unit: 2B Plants and animals in the local environment

Literacy objectives: Y1 T2 T19 • Y2 T3 T13, 14 • Y3 T1 T17 *Reading non-fiction, using non-fiction books to answer questions*

Ask the children what they know about ladybirds. They will probably say that they are red. Ask them if they have seen ladybirds in any other colour, and encourage them to use information books to find out the answer. Ask the children to find pictures of ladybirds and count their spots, recording the different types they find. They can write the information they find on the project. You could also ask them to find out why ladybirds are helpful to farmers and gardeners.

Discuss the fact that a ladybird is an insect. Ask the children if a human is an insect, and how they can tell. Discuss whether other familiar animals are insects, such as a dog and a sparrow. As an introductory activity to learning about insects, give the children a collection of pictures of animals and ask them to work in groups, dividing their sets of pictures into two sets: insect and not insect. Compare the groupings and ask the children how they decided which set to put an animal into. Point out that an insect has six legs and may have wings. Its body has three parts. Ask them to rearrange their sets of animals, asking the questions, 'Does it have six legs?' and 'Does its body have three parts?' Compare the groupings again and discuss any discrepancies. Point out that young insects usually look different from adult insects.

Pop-up bee (pages 43–44)

Science unit: 2B Plants and animals in the local environment

Literacy objectives: Y1 T1 T14 • Y1 T2 T22 *Writing labels*

To introduce the project, give the children some honey to taste. Ask them if they know what it is and where it comes from. Show them a video or a picture of bees in a hive and explain how bees make honey using pollen and nectar collected from flowers. Then talk about how people collect honey from hives, purify it and put it into jars for people to buy. Ask the children if they know why beekeepers need to wear protective clothing, and talk about the parts of a bee's body. Explain that the sting is at the very end of the body and provide reference books to help the children label their pop-up bees. For further work on bees, you could show the children a close-up of a honeycomb. Discuss how the bees make it from a material which they produce in their bodies — beeswax. You could also talk about how bees help plants to grow seeds by carrying pollen from one flower to another.

I spy an animal (pages 45–46)

Science unit: 2B Plants and animals in the local environment

If possible, take the class to visit a park or other habitat near the school. Explain that the place itself is a habitat, but it can be split into smaller habitats such as a bush, part of a wall and so on. Encourage the children to examine the smaller habitats and make notes about the animals they find. They can then use reference books to help them draw the animals on their scenes. Let the children look at one another's completed scenes to try to find all the animals and say what they are.

Animal secrets book (pages 47–48)

Literacy objectives: Y1 T1 T11 • Y1 T2 T17 • Y1 T3 T14 • Y3 T3 T10 *Fiction and non-fiction, writing simple picture book, writing stories based on reading*

Before beginning the project, discuss the difference between fact and fiction. Explain that there are true reasons for why animals are the way there are: for example, a monkey has a long tail to help it move through trees more easily. Then explain that for this project they are going to make up stories, or fiction, about how animals came to have certain features. You could read Rudyard Kipling's *Just So Stories* with them. The children may find it helpful to draft their stories on a separate piece of paper before copying them into the book. As an extension activity, ask the children to find facts about how the animals use the body parts. They could also investigate features of other animals, such as a whale's baleen or a snake's dislocating jaw.

Once I saw… (pages 49–50)

Literacy objectives: Y1 T2 T16 • Y3 T2 T9 *Writing based on stories read, writing myths*

Read stories about fictitious animals such as unicorns and dragons, and show the class pictures of them. Ask the children to notice which parts of these animals resemble parts of real animals. They are likely to find that most fictitious animals are made up of parts which can be found on real animals, but not all on the same one. Encourage the children to gather ideas for their invented animal by combining parts of different familiar animals. They should make notes about the animal's body parts and what it does. Suggest that they consider how the animal hunts and how it defends itself. Provide a range of collage materials such as foil, cling film, wool, broken eggshell and so on, so that the children can experiment with textures for their animal's skin.

Animal factfile (pages 51–52)

Science unit: 2C Variation — *Observing simple characteristics of animals*

Literacy objectives: Y1 T2 T17 • Y2 T3 T13 • Y3 T1 T17 *Fact and fiction*

Before beginning, discuss the meaning of 'facts'. Ask a child to choose an animal (without saying its name) and give a fact about it. Let the child continue giving facts until one of the others can identify the animal. Provide information books about animals and encourage the children to use the headings on their factfiles to focus their research. On pages 6 and 7 they could record whether the animal is nocturnal or diurnal, how it hunts, whether it spends most of its time alone or in a group, whether it migrates or travels long distances, and so on.

Quiz book (pages 53–54)

Science unit: 2C Variation — *Observing simple characteristics of animals*

Literacy objectives: Y1 T3 T19 • Y2 T3 T14 *Questions and answers*

Each child or pair of children could make a quiz book for a different animal. The children need to be able to answer their questions in one or two words; they should plan the questions on scrap paper to check this is possible. Questions that can be answered yes or no are ideal. The completed quiz books could be used for an interactive library display for other children to visit.

Research file (pages 55–56)

Science unit: 2C Variation — *Observing simple characteristics of animals*
Literacy objectives: Y1 T2 T21 • Y2 T2 T18 • Y2 T3 T15 • Y3 T1 T19 • Y3 T3 T17 *Using an index, locating information*

Provide a range of appropriate books, CD-ROMs and website addresses, and a supply of extra 'pages' measuring approximately 8.5 cm x 6.5 cm. Encourage the children to write open questions: for example, ones beginning 'how' or 'why'. Remind them to abbreviate words when making notes, and to miss out words such as 'a' and 'the'. The children could think of key words connected with their questions and look up these key words in the index of a book. Some children may find it helpful to write the key word on a slip of paper and then move it down the index until they find the matching word. Before they do this, ask them whereabouts in the index they will begin looking (for example, if they are looking for 'moth' they should start at 'm'). Extra pieces of information can be added to the file at a later date, as the children come across them.

Glossary of animal parts (pages 57–58)

Science unit: 2C Variation — *Observing simple characteristics of animals*
Literacy objectives: Y1 T2 T20 • Y2 T2 T20 • Y3 T3 T24 *Alphabetical texts*

For this project it will be useful to revise alphabetical order, including the second letters of the word. Some children might be able to arrange words alphabetically by the first three letters. The children also need to have had experience of using glossaries. Talk about the purpose of a glossary and how it is different from an index. Discuss what a definition is. With the children, read some dictionary definitions of animal parts and talk about the way in which they are written: they need not be complete sentences. Point out the ways in which the head words are made to stand out from the rest of the text to make them easy to read: they are usually in bold or enlarged type, or even in colour.

Before the children write their glossary they need to count how many words they can fit into it and then make a list of the animal parts they want to include. They might have to omit some of them. Ask them which ones are the most important. Different children could include different animal parts, so that between a group as many as possible can be included. Once they have their final list, ask them to write each word on a slip of paper and then to arrange them in alphabetical order.

Useful contacts

You and your class can find extra ideas, information and pictures for the projects in this book by visiting the following websites or contacting the organisations below.

Websites

General
www.bbc.co.uk/nature
  Includes animal factfiles, photographs and quizzes.
www.uksafari.com
  Features photographs, facts and a newsletter.
www.wwf-uk.org
  The UK website for the WWF.
www.worldwildlife.org/fun/kids.cfm
  The WWF website for children.
www.wwflearning.co.uk
  Education resource website for the WWF.
www.kidsplanet.org
  Includes useful animal fact sheets.
www.zoo.org
  Seattle zoo website with photographs and webcams.
www.abdn.ac.uk/mammal/
  Website for the UK Mammal Society.
www.thebigzoo.com/
  Virtual zoo with detailed information.
www.nhm.ac.uk
  The Natural History Museum website.

Insects
www.insecta.com
www.bugbios.com
  Both provide detailed information suitable for teachers.

Birds
www.rspb.org.uk
  RSPB website with information, webcams and games.

Pets
www.mypetstop.com
www.rspca.org.uk
  Both provide information on caring for pets.

Links
www.educationplanet.com
netvet.wustl.edu
www.kidsites.com/sites-edu/animals.htm
  All offer links to animal-related websites.

Addresses

WWF – UK
Panda House
Weyside Park
Godalming
Surrey GU7 1XR
Tel: 01483 426444

National Geographic Society
P. O. Box 19
Guildford
Surrey GU3 3NY
Tel: 020 7365 0916